Building a Kingdom for Good In Our World Today

Building a Kingdom for Good In Our World Today

The Longbow Horseman Enterprise

CHRISTOPHER D IORG

Library of Congress Control Number: 2019921064

HARDBACK: 978-1-951461-93-5
PAPERBACK: 978-1-951461-92-8
EBOOK: 978-1-951461-94-2

Ordering Information:

For orders and inquiries, please contact:
1-888-404-1388
www.goldtouchpress.com
book.orders@goldtouchpress.com

Printed in the United States of America

CONTENTS

PREFACE

I wrote this book to empower as much good as I can in all that we can; with an amazing investment strategy that builds all the good things in our world today.

You will see these are more than lucrative business modules; these are critical infrastructure projects we can build all over our world today.

These modules will pay out in a lot of financial, spiritual, and worldly ways where everyone is empowered naturally to create a good life for ourselves and empower others to live a good life as well.

These modules and ideas create a world filled with better choices and opportunities that will fundamentally build our individual and collective responsibility throughout all parts of our lives, jointly all the time, similar to how public utilities empower all of us. A good way to look at this whole campaign is to understand these are the outlines of the 5 key blueprints that can build critical infrastructure in our world today.

Like any book, these words are meant to empower your imagination with valuable information. This book isn't just words and ideas for you to think about. This instant is a very exciting time for you because you're about to earn and learn the Greatest, most Peaceful, Loving, Unite-full, Respectful, Responsible and of course, the most Lucrative campaign ever speculated. How and why I want to claim this fact is the same reason why any good entrepreneur/ salesman wants to sell you the best possible deal where everyone can profit, and when I talk about profit I'm talking about a whole lot more then everyone being able to earn a lot of money. I'm staking this claim because it's the truth proven with simple math and because I don't want to sell anyone short on the best possible deal; which is how amazing our lives can be together in our world today, I can only guarantee for certain good results. How good it is up to you.

You will see there are plenty of real investment opportunities for you in these modules. If you are interested in learning more, all you have to do is email us longbowhorseman@gmail.com and tell us what you think. I will do my best to reply to you myself, but someone from our team will reply to you as soon as we can. Regardless of what you may think or say we will listen and do our best to take your advice, hear you, and reply to you as soon as we can.

These ideas and modules I'm about to describe are simple solutions we all have in common; by design, they will naturally steer maybe all, probably most, but for sure a great deal of individual and collective responsibilities in the right direction.

To understand what I'm talking about is to understand the rewards of practicing good behavior. We can all naturally be good human beings individually; collectively just like fish and birds naturally sync up together to most effectively move forward in the direction they want to go together.

The terminology for defining good behavior we categorize under principles. There are many good principles we should understand and practice. However, I will be highlighting five of our fundamental core principles into an already known acronym "P.L.U.R.R." Peace, Love, Unity, Respect, Responsibility. These principles are the core guidelines that ensure trust and guarantee the success of this campaign.

The modules I described are the key infrastructure projects that can empower everybody in everyone's own way, where we can all get along, with freedom to follow our hearts with an understanding whatever it is we decide to do with our time; we can all invest in making the world a better place in our own ways, fueling that which is good for life to grow. In other simple terms, these modules will empower people to become more intelligent, enlightened, and passionate in all the good things life has to offer. So, when and where these modules are built we the people will be empowered with good choices to build our kingdoms however we want; in an overall collective responsible manner where we all work together to make our world a better place!

Let this be known.

SUMMARY

Here are the outlines for each module so you have an idea of what I'm talking about before we get serious about our real problems. I want you to see how and where each of these modules can be our solution, all over our world today. Keep in mind these are well-thought-out, they work together like key infrastructure projects.

The first business module I want to share with you is called Free Water Marketing. This is a simple "cause" marketing strategy and one of the clearest ways to advertise a message. This module is designed to perpetually grow a worldwide charitable drinking water supply that empowers people to drink more water. This module earns a profit by growing other businesses by connecting them with their target market during special events. By wrapping a high-quality label advertisement around many individual nontoxic biodegradable water bottles and then by strategically donating those thousands of water bottles, we can create fertile branding conditions that grow profits for all parties.

Each advertisement is a gift, each advertisement moves with individuals for a long period of time, each advertisement directly goes in the face and can be seen by others, the bottle will be safe to reuse and nontoxic when it's no longer a viable water container (the nontoxic biodegradable water bottle is still to be determined), the label advertisement can use many different advertising strategies including traceable QR codes and coupons.

Before I started writing this book, I started Free Water Marketing in Salt lake Utah. I have much more detail I can share with you about this module if you are interested in directly getting involved in this project.

Free Water Marketing provides all the services required for any size business to grow simply by giving people what we need most during valuable times of our lives, - pure drinking water; that is the first simple business module of this campaign, which provides us with a great deal of profit we can use as capital to fund the rest of these modules.

From above, this module makes sense because we will be empowering people to drink water more often. From below, listening to someone who just explained how we can all invest in a way we can build a worldwide perpetual freshwater source that empowers everyone to drink more water; raises a great deal of profit for all parties is a good indicator your being lead in a direction you can trust towards health, growth, and prosperity.

The second module is a 21st-century Rental Bike Process that makes renting a bike far more convenient. This module empowers people to do physical exercise more often, in a fun way that gets you to where you want to go. This strategy also creates a major influence in our health care industry and empowers our public transportation systems.

By designing and programming hardware and software into a compact durable computer device that can mount on any bicycle, users can quickly log-in, ride the bike wherever, no matter how long they want at a low cost. When users are ready to return the bike the farthest they return it is near any bus route, quickly and easily by finding a safe place for the bike to park, the device will help with finding parking, basically, next to any responsible pole or bike rack; then pull the retractable cord around the pole and plug it back into its self-tight, which holds the bike upright and automatically logs the user off.

The device will keep track of many stats like how many calories we burned, distance traveled, how much money we saved, provide navigational tools, bus routes, train schedules, and more; if riders choose to enroll with our health insurance plans they will receive the very best health insurance and be able to earn health credits for every mile they cycled.

We can see how creating this computer device and branding with this rental bike process we can help people find the very best health insurance; it begins to fix our problems with our healthcare system directly. In chapter 1, I will describe how we can find and or create the best health insurance.

This third module changes everything for the better and nearly solves our entire world's economic problems; - it's called Make It Count. This programs functions are similar to the world of recruiting professional athletes. Except this program, works for everybody as our collective 21st-century resume builder.

This program will empower all of us to find professional and educational opportunities in a fundamental way that we choose to pursue. So, now with the Make It Count program we will be truly free to pursue our heart's passions. The Make It Count program empowers us to be able to record and organize what we learned about our day, building our resumes, then based on what we would like the world of opportunity to see is how we would want to build our resume.

If we can record and upload some evidence of our life experience today, then the question is how can we leverage our experience to find the best opportunities available today? That's what the Make It Count program does. It turns all your life experience into real-time tangible wealth and riches in many spiritual and worldly ways that you rightfully earn.

I will go into further detail on how it all works in Chapter 5 but the Make It Count program does exactly what the name says by connecting the individual with education and a purpose or profession. This program creates a way for everyone to know where to find the best job opportunity, the best employee, and the best way to leverage our education experience. The investor side of the Make It Count program empowers employers to find the best people for the job building better teams for our businesses. This is a critical investment because building better teams to grow our business ideas is how we build our critical infrastructure. Building and participating in this program is how we naturally overcome our individual and collective obstacles.

Everyone with valuable skills will be empowered to find better professional opportunities to provide for ourselves and our families. If we don't have enough skills to get the job we want and be passionate in that what we do, the Make It Count program will help us find educational opportunities that will help us learn the skills you need for the profession you desire.

The main application most people will use I'd imagine is the user-friendly smart camera phone application that helps transfer our life experience onto our Make It Count profile resume.

The Make It Count program allows us, individuals, to search and be found by future professional and educational opportunities, which is based on our honest opinion of our life experience and ability to translate our experience onto our Make It Count profile. Recording our accomplishments will help us go back into our past and reflect, remember, and grow further knowledge and skills just by being able to look back at what we learned and experienced in our past. This will help us reflect, review, remember, our past in the present to better our future.

Finding purpose and meaning in our lives is the momentum we can use to build our kingdoms, especially when we are financially and spiritually rewarded for investing in good things. This is how we turn our valuable time into good money earned, which is as good as gold!

The Make It Count program is Alchemy at its finest because we aren't talking about turning lead into gold. We are talking about wisely turning each of our days' worth of valuable life experience into tangible real-time long term assets that buy things like freedom, purpose, and passion that resembles the same physical qualities gold and silver have in our lives.

This fourth part is an investment strategy called Keys for Freedom. This idea is investing in the spread of knowledge in the form of positive useful information. Nowadays, we know this as the spread of information via the Internet; so we will do our best at that and also invest in the hard copy version of distributing information, which means we will invest a great deal in our public libraries, museums, and preserving significant archeological sites.

This fifth module is nonprofit and is where we will spend a lot of the money earned from the other modules. It's called the Community Project House. This is a 21st-century hands-on college that teaches lessons through community projects.

The first roll-out community project will be the community garden project. This project is our long term front where anyone can volunteer to serve the people in a long term fundamentally empowering uniting way; we will need to build and or partner with local governments, established community gardens and schools to teach these lessons on a global scale.

Depending on what our individual goals are and what needs to be done in that community, the common focus is communicating with people in ways that build friendships involved with building the critical infrastructure project.

The reason why people will want to be friends with our missionaries is that they will have a great deal of power and resources behind them to help make people's lives better. While we are working together during and between the projects we will talk to each other, learn about each other's ideas, understand each other's differences, and have as much fun as we can while accomplishing the goals of the project.

The first projects that will be approved for funding will be building critical infrastructure. Since we need our bodies healthy and strong, I figured the first infrastructure project should be investing in properties all over the world that can be grown into indoor and outdoor community gardens. Then we will need to create an organization to recruit, train, and send people on missions to these facilities all over the world to find hungry people and bring them back to the garden. So the people can practice and learn some of the most valuable lessons which are how to grow food properly, feed ourselves and others; as time goes on, depending on each garden's ability to grow, so will the funding for more advanced community projects.

After we have established growing community gardens and if there are enough people in that community to take on another project, then we can arrange a project or they can submit their own proposed idea, and we at the main campuses will approve, arrange, and send resources to the front all over the world all the time. One of the biggest qualifying grants for funding is when a community project is working with the local education system. We will design these projects like a public workshop, where we supply everything needed for teachers to take their students on a field trip and teach hands-on lessons with real applications.

PROLOGUE

I've been writing and building these business modules since 2012. I wrote this book because I believe to have discovered the entrepreneurial blueprints to build a kingdom for all that is good here on earth today. Believe it or not, all you have to do is read this book, understand these simple business modules assume we can learn from our mistakes and build these ideas with wise business practices, and you will know for yourself how this amazing claim is true. By the time you're done reading this short book, you will know the outline to the greatest, most lucrative campaign for all that is good our civilization has ever speculated.

That being an answer said, what are some questions we should all ask to understand our greatest individual and collective obstacles in our world today? Are the obstacles the same as they have always been or are they different? Is our greatest collective obstacle weather and Mother Nature's natural disaster nature? What is it we all have to figure out every day, especially, to be a productive member of your community as an adult?

Is it a must that we all figure out how we can thrive in harmony with each other, with all the plants, animals and resources that exist in our environment every day?

The best way we can survive and thrive in the world today is by understanding how to apply good principles in our lives. Here are some examples of how we can use principles. We must live peacefully with each other. We must do our best to love all that we can, love ourselves, love as many people as we can and earn love from as many people as we can, love to learn, love your job, and love persevering through hard times especially by practicing good principles. We must live united together as an intelligent enlightened human species and understand our actions have a great impact on our environment just like our environment has a great impact on us. We must be respectful of all by being as honest as we can and practice empathy for others. We must do our best at being responsible for our actions and doing our best at responding when we can do something good.

Since money is the tool we all pretty much have in common, then we must seek to understand the rules behind money. Seek to earn money positively. Find out what our taxes are being invested in making sure we are fueling that which is good for life to grow. We should make sure our money fuels good things that are relatively peaceful, made and used with love, unifying, respectful, and responsible. An example of what I mean by relatively peaceful is anything can be used to harm someone but is it designed for a peaceful application? Is it something people love? Is it available and safe? Does it respect the laws and life in its environment? What are the responsible instructions for its use and disposal? These are some examples of how we can apply the principles behind our money.

I will get into how we can influence good change in our collective currency in later chapters because the simple solution is to apply good principles behind our laws and currencies on an individual level.

That idea I just explained is not that complicated, most of us and our laws and money act by these principles naturally already.

Anytime we want to propel our lives forward in a positive direction regardless of what is going on around us is by practicing these principles within our thoughts and actions, and by the laws of the universe, we are guaranteed to get to where we want to go. Practicing good values and principles is what can unite all of us together regardless of what language we speak, or whatever it is we decide to do with our time, we can all agree we should go about it with the understanding of how to apply principles throughout our lives.

We can create a simple solid category rating system using these 5 principles: Peace, Love, Unity, Respect, and Responsibility, because of the violent nature that exists in our lives, whether it's violence from an accident, fighting with each other, killing plants and animals for our food, and especially our threat from collective natural disaster violence. The point being, peace is not always achievable in all aspects of our environment; at times we will break some of these principles. That makes applying all the other principles the best we can critical to justify and be responsible for our actions.

We can see how we have working governments with law enforcement practices. How we protect ourselves and watch over the watchers is by understanding how to apply the P.L.U.R.R. principles over all laws, policies, and actions, so naturally we the people will find the best solutions.

What this idea looks like in our banks and governments is basically by reviewing how well laws, policies, programs, and decisions apply in each of the P.L.U.R.R principles. For example, we can simply apply a five-star gold, silver, bronze category rating system with a minimum standard. So, if your business module makes decent sense in these categories then you have a legal business module. Most businesses in our world already do their best to operate under these principles. The business modules that take risks that conflict with these principles will be either illegal or confronted with more strict laws, and regulations, which is kind of what happens already.

As far as all of our collective efforts together can influence, life as we know it will never be perfect or easy for us individually, but we can all do our part to create, empower, and build our collective kingdom in a way that empowers everyone's collective responsibilities.

Applying these business modules will only empower more, if not all of us, to better our lives and overcome our collective obstacles that are in our future.

THE HEALTH CARE ACT

The first problem I want to address is the one in our health care system. The problem is when we get diagnosed by a doctor, likely, we will only be offered a pharmaceutical drug remedy. Not all pharmaceuticals are bad but we can all agree there are too many bad drugs prescribed to millions of children and adults of all types that can be scientifically proven as unnecessary and filled with many risks and harmful effects.

The solution to this problem is amazing and our healthcare industry is already prepared for this change, many of the best solutions to our health problems can be found by local businesses that already exist. The change that needs to happen is through insurance policies, by creating incentives for our doctors to prescribe the best solution to their patients' health problems, especially, if there are low-risk behavioral forms of treatment available. So, between you and your health care provider, you can come up with a health recovery plan which is a combination of things that the patient understands and agrees to do.

Depending on the case, there will be a combination of behavioral practices; maybe a combination of pharmaceuticals and other alternative medicines. All of which the patient can seek to understand until agreed upon that these prescribed remedies are good for health recovery plan. If and when you and our Healthcare provider succeed at getting back to health or back on a healthy recovery, then our healthcare providers earn a tax-free bonus on the back end with a lump sum or a long term monthly payment plan guaranteed by the health insurance.

That paragraph you just read will flip the incentive process around in our healthcare system so health care providers are incentivized to prescribe the very best remedies to our health issue, not only that but creating that process will flow billions of dollars throughout the entire economy supporting all good health care practices. We will all love this change especially our doctors, the more people Doctors heal pro-actively for the long term the less they might have to work in their future to keep earning cash flow because of how many people were healed correctly in the past.

The only ones affected negatively by this change are people and organizations who have been investing their time and money in harmful drugs. Therefore, we should not hear any complaints, all they would have to do is start investing in good drugs and healthy behavior remedies and they will see a positive return of investment.

Our current FDA policies are somehow systematically creating paths for the pharmaceutical industry to sell unnecessary drugs that come with a high-profit margin, many serious risks, and harmful effects. The sad part is it's happening in the name of extremely large amounts of money which swells and inflames parts of the industry to control parts of our government, which it is today in America, not necessarily all over the world. It's sad because selling the best ways to heal our bodies would still drive a great profit for everyone involved and they deserve every penny.

The answers to most of our health care system are simple to understand. First of all, we know our bodies heal themselves based on a lot of factors but our bodies fundamentally heal themselves, and it's our health care provider's job to heal our body's healing process depending on the circumstance. Also, think about how the placebo effect is scientifically proven and works. We can heal ourselves just by believing we have what we need to be healed. If the harmful drugs we might be consuming seem to work that's probably because we **believe** our bodies are receiving what it needs to be healed. But in fact, we are better off starting our healing process fundamentally by believing in ourselves, thinking good thoughts, and adjusting our behaviors right now. Sometimes, high-risk drugs seem to help with symptoms we may have but more than likely they are just trying to cover up the problem, the risks are probably not worth it, there is likely a natural drug remedy with little to no risks to solve our same health issue.

The best way to proactively heal the masses minds and bodies every day is by empowering them in these categories as much as is necessary for the individual, the basic way we can do that is by informing people with the right healthy information. Like how important a natural good night sleep is, Learn about good things we should ingest into our bodies on a daily basis, including how and when it's appropriate to practice not eating "fasting" properly. Other examples is how much vitamins and minerals we should include in our diets, the types of foods that include the types of vitamins and minerals we should eat, the specific exercise routines we should perform, etc. There are many different good ways to go about living a healthy life and we all get to choose our own way regardless so why not create empowering choices we all want to make regardless.

Our health care providers should be able to prescribe us with helpful resources available for us to heal ourselves, especially if there is a local business that provides the remedy we might need. A good example is right now there is a wide variety of professional behavioral medicines that already exist but are cut off from a great deal of our health insurance dollars. A few examples we may already know about, are personal health trainers, nutritionists, chiropractic, acupuncture, yoga, weight training, guided hiking trips, etc. The problem is our health insurance often doesn't pay for these. That might be because often our doctors don't prescribe these correct healthy behaviors and medicines because there is no incentive for them to do so; simple healthcare laws and policies that can be changed. At the end of this chapter, I put together some legislative language into a draft that we can use to get talking about these ideas and start to tell the right people who can pass a bill into law. If you see corrections or better words to use or anything to improve this language into a bill that can be made into law, please write it down and email us what you would change and why.

By empowering doctors with incentives to prescribe behavioral remedies they believe will help heal their patients, including the good forms of pharmaceutical drugs, and if health insurance will guarantee healthcare providers fair payment and help cover other costs, that would dramatically stimulate the whole health care system and our entire economy.

Our healthcare system already performs a lot of the things that are good for us; we just need to stop doing the bad stuff. How we can go about doing that is, like I said creating incentives for our doctors to provide us with a lot more, if not all, the best possible ways to heal our minds and bodies.

By changing the insurance process, when people get sick and our healthcare system pro-actively heals us, then the patient owes the health care practice a fare lump sum or long term monthly payment plan which is guaranteed by our health insurance.

If patients are given the all-natural and behavioral medicine choice to heal ourselves right next to the high-risk cover up the problem pharmaceutical stuff, then our health care system would be empowering us with a choice and we would have an empowering choice to be able to choose for ourselves the type of health care we want to receive.

We, the people need to demand that our food and drug laws get straighten out; we need to build incentives to make sure our doctors prescribe us with the very best information and behavioral forms of medicine just about every time we go into the doctors. It's very likely we could always use some sort of empowerment often throughout our entire life. We already have a lot of amazing good drugs out there including the science behind the natural remedies, and many of the legal alternative medicine businesses already exist, so our health care system is already prepared to solve this problem.

There are many millions of people who are systematically being tricked into ingesting high-risk harmful substances. However, these drugs get distributed especially to the masses is a strategic chemical attack against our people and easily one of our greatest security issues. It's ok if these drugs exist and scientifically studied, it's not ok for companies to distribute these harmful drugs on a massive scale seriously harming millions of our citizens regularly. Talking this way about harmful drugs are facts that all of us understand, we all likely have our own personal testimony of experiencing the harmful effects of bad drugs.

Our health care system keeps track of a lot of the evidence; we can see the numbers very well that prove this claim.

The minor conflict with this claim is that it will stop billions of monthly cash flow dollars from going to powerful corporations that have been investing in these drugs. The reality though for these enormous corporations is, they don't come close to the size and responsibility of the United States Government which is bound to protect the people. Changing a few simple healthcare laws that will fix our health care system, empower our doctors and lighten their future workload, heal everyone far better, and stimulate the entire economy the right way with a few tax dollars is a win for everybody. This bill is one of those that are so beneficial to the American people that whoever doesn't vote for it is going to be on the wrong side of history.

We live in the land with the greatest amount of opportunities and freedom, because a few good men and women a long time ago did their best to come together to become great. They simply wrote down the best words they could agree on at the time and declared it on this land we are standing on, which holds the greatest powers of all with the purpose to protect those few good words that can be found in the United States Constitution, our Bill of Rights, and many other documents and policies that our government is empowered by.

Those words happen to empower all of us with a precise power for anyone to stand up for what's right and sling peaceful paperwork to take down giant evil corporations in this country.

I don't think all drugs are bad, some of them work and make sense, and I believe most of our doctors do a great job with what they have to work with. Our healthcare system already does a lot of what they should be doing, we need to cut out the bad stuff before it spreads and gets any worse.

We should easily be able to stand up for what we know is right about our health care system; we all get sick and we all need health care, therefore, if we make our health care system great, life for all of us will get so much better and going to the doctors will be worth everyone's time and money.

LEGISLATION DRAFT - BILL PROPOSAL

The United States Health Care Act
Long Bow Horse Man Enterprise, LLC

This bill will save millions of American lives and redirect the flow of billions of health insurance dollars that are currently going to high-risk harmful drugs, and uses that money to empower health care providers with incentives to heal their patients with exactly what each patient may need for a healthy recovery.

That means Health care providers can design or refer to any healthy medicine or behavioral functioning mean that acts as a medicine/therapy to their patients as part of a formally prescribed health recovery plan.

This bill keeps all the good stuff about our health care system but flips the incentive system around so our insurance providers reward health care providers on how well they heal people.

If the patient neglects to follow the agreed-upon health action plan, then if future health costs go up from the patient not practicing good behavior in the agreement, insurance providers can be less responsible for their patients' health recovery costs, depending on the patient's case and agreed upon insurance plan.

Doctors and health care providers who pro-actively heal patients in ways their patients live long healthy lives, both the patient and health insurance providers will guarantee a monthly healthy patient fee on top of their health recovery prescription plans and depending on other overhead costs. Both families and individuals paying for health insurance each month will guarantee fare monthly payments to their health care providers each month they are healthy, especially if the patient recovered from serious health issues.

This bill lowers the long term cost and raises profits for all parties including the patient, insurance provider, and health care provider; because often the best things for our health recovery are inexpensive. So patients will be empowered with a lot more healthy insurances when paying for health insurance.

Some examples of what health insurance will cover, Gym membership / personal trainer, yoga/stretching class, meditation courses, group therapy sessions, one on one psychologist sessions, spas/massages, chiropractor, acupuncture, you name it, basically anything that makes sense to you and your doctor that will help your recovery.

These next definitions are examples to categorize drugs by risk.

Definitions of high-risk harmful drugs are those that consistently prove to seriously harm a patient's mind and or body, especially when there is a known lower risk healthy alternative to the same health issue.

Definitions for medium risk drugs are those that could have 5 or more minor effects on the mind or body but none are serious. Or if less than 3 serious effects may happen in a small number of patients and no other known remedy is available.

Definitions of low-risk drugs are those that have 5 or less minor effects on the mind and body none are serious.

To scale the difference of seriousness of harm of any particular drug is to compare results with patients who are treated first with the proper information, provided with dietary empowerment resources, and empowered with the proper exercise, and a doctor's note to get at least 7 hours of sleep.

1. Whereas high risk harmful drugs are legally prescribed to millions of our citizens on a regular bases when other known lower risk alternative medicine exists.

2. Whereas great amounts of evidence show many different high risks harmful prescription drugs are having many different harmful, lethal, and unnecessary effects on millions of Americans directly and their friends and family members indirectly.
3. Whereas the current laws and regulations on drugs is fueling all forms of destruction and poverty.
4. Whereas doctors and science already know the correct answers to the vast majority of health care issues and they can be healed fundamentally with the proper information, diet, exercise and sleep.
5. Whereas high risk harmful drugs cannot be justified as the correct remedy or solution to any individual health problem when other medium and low risk, better remedies exist.

High-risk harmful drugs cannot be prescribed by a health care provider for any patient's health recovery, especially when there is a scientifically proven low/medium risk alternative.

High-risk drugs maybe legal and accessible under controlled facilities, for whatever risk-seeking reasons people may have for these drugs, there will be a legal way for people to purchase and ingest these drugs at the controlled facilities. Participating in a high-risk substance program may harm individuals physically and disqualify them from future opportunities.

How we frame the communication between the individual patient, the health care provider, and the insurance provider is by focusing on the 3 main categories of healing people.

1. Quality of provided information, creating a value for the information the Doctor/ health care provider, including how it was provided / the whole experience while on a health care providers property has a value. So do the referrals they offer to other health care providers, educational courses, any licensed business that has a product or service involved with healing can be considered on the patient's health action plan.

   ➢ This allows health care providers to include the cost in the quality of information they provided to their patients. Because insurance providers want the best information provided to their patients, and patients want the best answers to their questions.

   ➢ This will create the demand for the best current information to be provided to us as patients; however, not every patient wants all available information. So, naturally, how much information provided is based on the health care provider and the questions asked by the patient. If the healthcare provider can't provide a correct answer they can't include it on the bill, but they can refer you to someone who can find the answer you're looking for and if the patient does find help then your health care provider can collect a small healthy referral fee.

   ➢ Formal surveys may be required for patients to fill out during and after treatment for proper billing. Both healthcare providers and insurance providers about the whole experience.

2. All dietary empowerment including high-grade prescription food that contains the remedy, also low-risk pharmaceutical supplements, all blood, mind, and body analysis, and webcam or onsite nutritionist for guided dietary empowerment.

➢ This creates a demand for high-quality food to be grown and distributed to people who get a prescription from their doctors to do so. However, this is not a financially viable long term solution for the patient to eat healthily. These are specially grown and preserved foods for health care providers to prescribe as a special order to get their patients back to health.

➢ Doctors can still prescribe all low-risk positive drugs, vaccines, vitamins, and supplements with full incentives.

➢ Doctors may prescribe Medium risk drugs without healthier alternatives but they come with limited incentives.

3. All physical and mental exercise empowerment including referrals to any prescribed licensed businesses that provide the proper health care practice for the patient's remedy. Examples are many different local businesses that already exist: yoga classes, meditation classes, chiropractic, mental health therapists, acupuncture, massage therapy, culinary classes, and guided outdoor hikes. Any legal business product or service that a doctor understands to be the remedy for their patient can be written as a prescription and covered by insurance providers.

➢ This creates incentives for doctors to refer patients to other health care providers.

➢ This allows health care providers to expand their services into many other means of healing people and earning money.

➢ This stops billions of dollars from flowing to harmful drugs and directs billions of dollars to many millions of local businesses that will thrive from our guaranteed health insurance dollars and stimulating our lives and our economy in many ways.

➤ The only people who lose by these bills passing are ones who invested in bad drugs which have proven to produce bad results.

➤ Because of the epidemic results these many harmful drugs are having on the American people today and across the world for many decades now. The people and organizations who fight this bill without good reason or continue the distribution of these harmful drugs illegally could go under investigation and be prosecuted for serious crimes against humanity.

➤ Because of the nature of a free market the people and organizations that have been designing, manufacturing, distributing harmful drugs may be forgiven if they support this bill and change their ways to follow these new laws and regulations.

➤ The people and organizations that help see this bill passed into law will be responsible for saving hundreds of millions of lives directly today and the entire world tomorrow.

➤ **How we can implement these ideas, regardless, is by selling health insurance that follows these ideals. See Chapter 4**

NOTES

CHAPTER 2

PAST PRESENT FUTURE

Before we get down to further details about the business, we should take some time to study and think about the past to see how far humanity has come. Get a good understanding of how we have improved from our past, and how we can continue to improve. We should use our imaginations to create a positive picture of what we would like our world to be, in the past, right now, our future, especially for our children. Write that down in your journal. We also need to realize we are all in this together. Some of us need to look far into the future but for now, let's focus on the 21st century, our lifetime, our kids, grandkids, and great-grandkids' near future; because we are fortunate to be alive today we all owe a great deal of gratitude to a lot of people in our past.

There are many ways we can learn from the past, by listening and learning from our elders, by reading a lot of good books, and simply by learning from our mistakes.

To give my answer to the earlier question about our future; I believe it is going to be great, far better than what most of us have imagined! Unfortunately, it doesn't have to be if we don't choose it so. I believe most of us are good people and sometimes great people under the circumstances. That's why a big part of humanity is continuing in a positive direction. I think that's because of the little good things we do for each other and the positive thoughts we feel, add up and go a long way. That's why we have created all that we have so far, now it's time, we, the people, the masses start acting like we know what we are doing to make our world a better place today.

When we see those who are lost and off-track, remember all that is required for them to find their hearts' path is a soft touch in the right direction. There is no better service than to help others, to find joy, passion, and love in their lives.

A soft touch in the right direction can radiate our love through our body by reaching out to help someone with our hands, words, actions, and resources.

When we help others, especially those who are lost, we get to learn from each other's experiences. So, the further off track we are or someone is that we get to know and help, the further our understanding grows which broadens our range of power and influence we can use tomorrow.

Truly helping others dramatically affects the whole in a ripple effect, greater then we can imagine. How we can plan an effective approach to help others on an individual level is to help them think about things they love, help them identify someone who loves them or even something they love, help them feel good thoughts or figure out something they can do to get their minds off themselves and explore ways they can show love and kindness to others, especially, to their children, family, and friends; from there gets you both off to a good start.

It takes good judgment to decide how much help someone might need because sometimes people don't want help or we can always try and help people, there's nothing wrong with that, but if we truly want to help others get to a better place in their lives, then we need to have a good understanding of the people we are trying to help. While at the same time, we should be on a joyful path, we need to consider where we have been, where we are now relative to where the person is who we want to help. That's why we want to get to know each other first, but that depends on our ability to ask each other the right questions and communicate effectively. It's better for us if we do this in person with emotions interacting together over long periods.

What I just said in a shorter term is called taking good advice. We learn best from people who have been where we are and are headed down the right path they believe they're meant to be on. Even if it's not necessarily the same path we want to be on; when someone is on their right track they usually have valuable advice to share with the world and we all should speak from our hearts and bare our testimonies to each other often.

Since we know the first few steps on how we can help others on an individual level, let's move on to how we can influence people on a collective level. First, we need to understand every single one of us can't help but change our environment with every breath and step we take. We all have to live on this planet together; we all have to live with each other's individual choices regardless of where we are and what the laws are. We all make choices that follow through with consequences that add up and create a collective result upon our environment which affects all of life everywhere on our planet.

To figure out the best ways to make the world a better place for the long run, let's ask some fundamental questions to find some fundamental answers. What are the basic things we all need just about every day to physically survive and thrive in our world today? Clean air to breath, food, water, shelter, education, helpful information, healthy diet, exercise, sleep, technological innovation, tools, a convenient way to get around, a purpose, a job to do, love in our lives, family, friends, many random others, a health care system, a smart government that does what's right for the people, faith, hope, organized institutions promoting positive religious traditions and that teach historical lessons, etc.?

Now, what is the best way to provide people with things that they need? - Through business processes of course. By Investing in these fundamental areas of life, through wise business strategies we can empower the masses in each critical area of life with clear enlightened choices that will lead us to a far better future.

So, we need to provide the masses with simple processes to follow including our sincere love and support along the way. But to steer clear and overcome the obstacles that lay ahead, I or we need to get things done right. A campaign plan like this will require a great deal of leadership that I would like to see come from everyone especially if you are aware of the golden rules.

The golden rules are both of these sayings put together in our hearts and minds. "Those whom have the gold with a good purpose make the rules". And "Do unto others that you would have them do unto you."

Now that we have covered the basics and have a better understanding of what the right answers will look like, let's get down to business!

CHAPTER 3

FREE WATER MARKETING

This first module is about delivering messages to people by giving away custom labeled water bottles to targeted audience. We make that possible by providing all the services needed for businesses to advertise on the labels; High-quality labels. Then we strategically donate the water to schools and event centers that hold sponsors' target market. Then the event staff sells and gives away the waters during and after events, directly reaching people on an individual level.

The label can include a coupon or promotional product so each water bottle advertisement holds several valuable and tangible marketing strategies that effectively reach the eyes of people who can see and appreciate our sponsors' water bottle as a gift of water we put in their hands, at the same time the advertisement is seen and appreciated and moves with them for a period of time. So, now businesses can brand more effectively and practically anywhere they want by giving people water. It's that simple.

There are many tangible marketing benefits with advertising around water bottles and giving it away, people appreciate businesses that show support in their community like schools, event centers. Giving people clean drinking water with a coupon is one of the best gifts we can come up with; we can give to anyone, any day, anytime, anywhere in the world.

We increase the value by creating ideal branding conditions. So, our clients can sponsor events exclusively for years at a time, repeatedly reaching the same targeted audience over and over.

The schools and local event centers around your business hold the families who consume products and services in your area; by showing them support during their children's special events by donating thousands of water bottles raises a lot of easy money for the school programs and get your business message out simply and effectively. So not only does each advertisement work but it's seen as a gift and appreciated which has direct tangible value to the school, event center, each person who receives water, us at FWM, and most of all our sponsors.

This is a simple way to grow company brands by showing people and events in our communities' support, it's cost-effective, any size business can afford to invest in these services because they can choose to keep some of the water to sell and give the rest away, both effectively advertising and minimizes the cost with a great chance of growing your business.

FWM staff provides all the services required through the process, creating exclusive sponsorship contracts with event centers, schools, festivals, practically anywhere, even a busy street corner.

These services I have mentioned, no other marketing company is providing; this is an entirely new advertising industry that could have existed for a long time now, designed to empower the world of business to earn profits by investing in pure drinking water, giving it away is strategically a big deal that will help ensure the survival of our people. Putting the world of business advertising dollars behind the amount of portable clean drinking water available for people to consume everywhere is a miracle that we can perform by investing in this module!

Many water bottle manufactures supply custom labeled water bottles, which are already established, which means we don't have to have a lot of capital to establish our services worldwide. But If it's possible I would like to invest in our water bottling and distribution process and use nontoxic biodegradable materials for our bottles.

The other application to this module is funding a foundation to provide natural disaster areas with water.

There is another application which will play a big part in influencing our government which is extremely valuable, political advertising. When people running for office get approved from us at the Long Bow Horse Man Enterprise everyone will know who we approve of to vote for because they will be on our water bottles.

When we look at the big picture, God and Mother Nature use water to shape the world, it makes sense advertising water is the best way for mankind to do the same. Water is the greatest resource to make life grow. It works the same way to grow our business profits by investing in people by giving them water with our brand around the label is the clearest way to advertise and grow our business.

This first business module is the fountain of money that clears the way for the rest of these modules to grow.

NOTES

CHAPTER **4**

RENT A BIKE

This second module is creating a mass transit rental bike system linked to Insurance companies and Public transportation systems. Rental bike processes already exist and we can partner with many of these already existing companies and use their bikes.

The problem with rental bike systems today is the capital requirements and pre-determined bulky return stations. Buying a personal bike requires capital most people don't have. A lot of people still don't ride a bike to work and school because it's not convenient enough. Plans change once you leave home on your personal bike, you're stuck with it.

This rent-a-bike process allows the user to rent the bike for long periods, able to take the bike anywhere, even overnight to their homes at a low cost. When the user is done, all they have to do is ride to the nearest bus route, find the nearest pole or simple bike rack, hook up the device and walk away. Creating freedom and allowing "change of plans" transitioning into a car possible, making the choice for people to ride our bikes to work and school much easier.

By designing a little computer device with the right software applications and a strong retractable cord system, we can turn any bike, new or used into a win/win lucrative traceable asset. The small digital device mounts safely on the bike allowing the user to quickly log in and rent the bike, after creating an online profile. The device offers computer functions that accurately records statistics for each user, automatically uploading onto their profile. Through the user's profile, they can make payments, manage their accounts, review their healthy lifestyle statistics like how many miles they have ridden, how many calories they burned, and about how much money they have saved compared to driving a vehicle. We will also create a phone application for people to locate nearby available bicycles and bus routes.

Without having to pay for the bulky return stations or the bikes the capital requirements we can minimize by leasing the devices out to local bike shop owners, allowing them to create long term monthly cash flow assets with a percentage of their inventory.

The majority of our profits will come from partnerships with health Insurance companies. That will require a partnership and pre-approved health insurance plans that we can sell and promote to the world, especially our riders. Because we will be referring millions of proactive healthy living people, who are willing and able to ride bikes directly to our partnered insurance agencies. That is extremely valuable at this moment in time. People will gain health credits for each mile they ride that helps pay for medical bills and users will be able to transfer these credits to other people in their plan and to anyone enrolled with our insurance agencies that are not able to ride bikes.

Just about every parent in the world will want to enroll in our health insurance programs and make their kids ride our bikes to school if it helps lower that monthly bill. I think this day and age, our kids having all this easy-going technology, I think implementing this process is a great way for us and our kids to get more exercise.

Our process and device prove and records each user's miles, proving to insurance companies a healthy lifestyle allowing people to participate in health credit saving programs. Similar to ones that already exists, they are fairly simple to implement into individual and family plans.

Bicycles work well with public transportation systems, so more people will also commute using bus and rail transportation to save time and energy between certain geographical points. I would love to partner with public transportation authorities because they will benefit from our services and help increase convenience and safety.

This process will empower the masses to live a healthy proactive lifestyle, saving time and money all through our life. In the same trip to work and school, we won't have to take on the liabilities of a vehicle, saving hundreds if not thousands of dollars every year, lower our health insurance cost in many ways like by applying earned credits for every mile cycled.

Exercising our hearts is essential to our survival and riding a bike can increase the amount of time we have in our lives. And most importantly people will ride our bikes because it's fun.

NOTES

CHAPTER

MAKE IT COUNT

This simple process and computer program is the answer to all of our economical ways of life and fixes most of our worlds' problems in an amazing way that empowers everyone with the freedom to build a good kingdom in our world today.

It's a 21st-century resume builder that empowers people to record positive attributes we earn throughout our day, especially during work and school. Why especially at work and at school? - Because if your employer or school also participates in the Make It Count program then we can attach trusted sources to the uploaded information. Our teachers at school and Supervisors at work are the people in our lives who are the most trusted source for our resumes; they already hold major responsibility for us as students and employees. So, the idea is to have a lot of our uploaded resume information to be confirmed by trusted sources like our current teachers and supervisors to add extra value and trust to our individual resume uploads.

How we technically do this is by programming software into a smartphone application so many possible smartphone tools can be used to upload resume experience. When individuals fill out their profiles and start uploading their resume information we can attract employers and schools to fill out their profile information.

The programming empowers the individual with complete control over their profile so that the individual can control the worldwide flow of opportunity around us today. We just don't have the infrastructure to see it or be found by it.

The program uses our individual resume information to empower employers to find the best people for the job, which is across the board, the most valuable service that exists because figuring out how to provide for ourselves and our families, especially with a positive passion, is the point of our survival. That's why politicians are always talking about creating new and better jobs because they know how much that means to people. This module answers the creating jobs question and changes it to which jobs do we want and what do we need to do to build the life we want.

Teachers and educational institutions are going to love the make it counts program, this module and processes will make going to school the best place for people to be to gain knowledge and valuable experience for our resumes. Imagine going to school knowing that what you accomplish today at school turns into a lifelong asset that goes to work for you your whole life. I would imagine this will help students find passion in learning and see how every day at school is a serious business and every day counts.

Resume builders and social media sites like this already exist with similar processes but so far no one has figured out the answer completely yet, that's because they don't include our education system and put the individual/ school/ business on the same page.

Picture the current processes social media sites use today combined with the recruiting rating system the athletic world uses to record and recruit student-athletes which turn them into professional athletes.

When students participate in school athletic programs there are processes in place to record hundreds of different attributes for every student-athlete as a team and individually. There are many different sports programs with thousands of different statistics, it's a fairly complex process but as we can see our education system does this very well. Recording and keeping track of a wide variety of different attributes for every student-athlete who participates. All of those stats get uploaded to be compared with all the other relative student-athletes, state and nationwide for those people to be found by opportunity.

When we look at the student-athlete process and programs that our education system uses today and has done for a long time now, how we compare, predict, and statistically prove how this Make It Count program will work beyond doubt; and why our government and our education system must approve of simply because we are already doing it. Which happens to be an amazing thing, and it goes to show just how much we can learn from sports.

Creating a worldwide statistical rating list of talented student-athletes is where professional athletic business and hire education facilities go to contact qualified candidates. That's why student-athletes are approached with a lot more opportunity than the equally valuable student engineer, computer programmer, and everyone else in class because there is a built-in process for students who desire to be athletes to follow. So, if by chance they are good at any particular skill in any of the many different possible athletic programs, that one thing they are good at and probably love doing can get them seen by better life-altering opportunities and seriously improve the chances of them succeeding in life! And our whole education system is backed up behind them while they are doing it!

Uploading positive attributes and resume information onto the internet is how opportunity can find us. Otherwise, we live in the world we have today where most of us are limited to finding a career and educational opportunities. The Make It Count program turns the table so we can all be found for the things we are interested in, have experience in, and good at.

The same reason why we continue to see athletes getting better and better along with the world records getting broke over time is because of the modules we have in place for athletes. The Make It Count program is the module that creates a natural evolving education system that will empower people to become smarter and excel in life. This program will create the communication that empowers freedom for everybody to create a good life. In other words when this module turns into infrastructure empowering our communities it will be easy for people to find good in our world today, which is to have choices to fallow our hearts and thrive in our environment at the same time.

Our world is filled with better opportunities and experiences for all of us. Uploading our 21st-century resumes onto the internet with the world of business and education opportunities constantly looking and waiting for all of us, no matter who we are, where we live, or what we are interested in doing that's legal. We will all be able to find opportunities out there we love to pursue with passion.

After we create the Make It Count program, at the very least, a lot more of us won't be held back by our environmental circumstances as much because we will know how we can focus on making ourselves better to then have a positive impact on our environment and make good changes for ourselves and others.

This process truly creates freedom for us to follow our hearts and pursue our lives' passion; always know you can find a job to provide for ourselves and our families throughout our entire lives.

We can see how fraud won't be a big issue because like 20th-century resume employers are still going to interview candidates to confirm their resume information. If the user's Make It Count profile information is fraudulent they will likely be found out during the interview process or shortly after. If a user is found out to be fraudulent on their uploads there will be a procedure that lowers that user's trustability attribute rating. Kind of like when users don't do business properly on eBay, except our users will be enrolled under their actual name and social security number.

Honestly participating in this program there is nothing to lose because it's voluntary, you can opt-out at any time, and users only upload positive attributes for things that show experience in things that they want to be noticed for.

The individual user profiles don't get to browse other user's profiles and to create a business entity profile you have to have a business license and be registered with the State and pay fees for our information services.

This day and age its normal practice for both the individual and entities to enroll in social media programs like this, given the popularity of the current social media sites today we can see how obtaining this information and acquiring millions of users to participate in this program is easier than ever.

How the details work: The first part to design is for us individuals, like we just talked a little bit about creating a 21st-century resume builder which is basically when we get a good grade on an assignment, or complete a project we would want to upload any necessary evidence onto our profile, depending on the class syllabus there will also be attributes every student may click on if they felt they earned them. That way, we know the attributes are related to the class or job we were working on, and when our teacher or supervisor confirms our post then it builds our resume, our statistical ratings go up on those particular attributes.

The second part is the business/project employer profile where employment requirements, project details, and experience required are uploaded.

The school profile is designed to empower teachers by having a class filled with good students. At the end of each class session or whenever the teacher permits, many if not all students will upload all possible positive resume information, either by scanning homework, taking pictures of it, writing descriptively, etc. All the accepted student info will be attached to their profiles, building their attributes over time, especially as their students excel in the future.

Our teachers already do these same processes when they grade our papers, so not many changes for our teachers except they will be teaching a class filled with students eager to learn, showing up on time, paying attention; with an understanding, every class session counts.

Every accomplishment in school that we experience can be confirmed by school staff. So, every day, every class, every test, everything a student is already graded on will count towards building their professional resume. Every time a student shows up to class on time especially for years at a time is valuable information for employers. Every homework assignment, group project, science project, all subject- matter, anything the school staff would normally record can be uploaded as experience and knowledge increasing that particular subject rating, empowering every student to be noticed for what we learn and accomplish in school.

When we submit our positive experience, it goes into a review processes where then our teacher and supervisor can quickly and easily review all the uploads and either click confirm or request more proof or further explanation why do you feel you earned those attributes that are in question that day? So sometimes we will need to further explain or prove what is in question or just move on and do better at that particular attribute next time.

At work it's the same idea, just take a picture of what you accomplished that day, record it in a video, write it in the description box, or if your company has secret stuff and you can't take pictures then it would be up to your company to provide the visual evidence for their employees' profiles.

I figure most posts will be clicking the preprogrammed daily attributes that our schools and employers want to keep track of, scanning our homework assignments and essays, and taking pictures and videos of the work we did on a project.

On the individual profile, there will be a detailed description box where we write down in our own words what we learned that day. Acting like a journal entry but keep in mind our future opportunity might look at all the details of our resume so we would only want to include things we are interested in getting noticed for and we would obviously want to be honest, not sound perfect, and use our own words, kind of like when we post how we feel about our day on other social media programs, we will want to write down some positive experiences we earned throughout the day that build our resume profile, everything we put on our Make It Count profiles will work to find opportunities for us throughout our entire lives.

The individual user only has to upload positive resume attribute information, anything that the individual does not want to include on their profile they don't have to, we don't write negative resumes for ourselves; we don't get hired for jobs based on what skills we don't have.

The individual profiles will have all kinds of different positive attribute ratings that prove many different skills they excelled at through their life, including pictures and videos, and properly documented projects, favorite written essays on the books that we read because nobody has to sign off on your handwritten essays, they automatically increase our literacy penmanship and a few other attribute ratings.

The rollout will have a period for new users to upload past experiences if they can prove it somehow, by uploading further evidence or by having a qualified teacher or supervisor to sign off on your detailed past resume experiences. Obviously, the value of the resume evidence all depends on how well people gather and upload much evidence as you can but if you don't have much or any that's fine, during open enrollment if you can get your current or previous employers to sign on your past experience, this will give older people with more experience a fair advantage in the world of opportunity.

Creating this process is how we can consistently improve the global economy for as long as there is internet, with a worldwide Make It Count program, no matter who we are, what we are good at, or passionate about, there are better opportunities out there for all of us.

A good example is if a student is below average but makes sure to show up to class on time and participate in school all day starting when they get into middle school, by the time the child graduates high school enrolled in this program, you can bet an average student with 6 years of great participation and punctuality attributes won't have any trouble finding a great career after high school.

Every user will be able to create a network profile with much different back up potential careers and future educational opportunities creating security and stability in their lives.

This program is the beginning of creating a self-evolving education system because this will create a higher demand for people to continue going to school and educating them to become smarter throughout their entire lives.

This will create exponentially more opportunities in the world for everyone because when millions of businesses fill out their profile, we, as the individual user will be able to research where the demands are for jobs and specific skills. including everything you need to know for you to get a job that you want and if your still a student you can pick your education courses more effectively, or we will know in real-time where all the opportunities are that we qualify for right now, near and far. Because our profile will say right on top of the profile page how many professional opportunities are available right now. So many of us will always know exactly where we can find a good job and provide for ourselves, our families, and others.

With the information we obtain from this program, we can connect the world in the right way. When students graduate from high school, they have a lot more information when deciding their future. Saving time and money connecting with higher education facilities and employment opportunities with the best options and finding careers in what we went to college for, and possibly obtain scholarships and contracts with careers, like we see happen with college athletes.

This program creates a more predictable stable workforce and extremely empowers entrepreneurs, investors, business owners, and government. We need this module in place immediately especially for us in the United States, this is the smartest way forward. And simply by empowering many of us to continue educating ourselves and follow our hearts, then naturally we will save the United States and the World,-exactly how everybody wants.

THE MAKE IT COUNT PROGRAM FUNCTION DESCRIPTIONS

Here is the description of steps to start describing some of the basic functions to give software engineers an idea of what we need to do to build this module. At this time, I know very little about coding and how the technology works; I want to empower as many 21st-century "scribes" as I can, people who know how to write computer code, program, design and build software and hardware applications.

1. Use this document to talk to computer programmers about designing this software application.
2. Build A Team.

   ○ Sign legal documents

3. Design Individual Profile.

   ○ Profile Pictures, personal info

   ○ Apply all upload information capabilities

   ○ Create lists of all attributes including definitions and examples of how to perform them

   ○ Create personal attribute stats, collective attribute stats, averages

○ Video tutorials on how to build resumes and properly document projects, how to use all other program tools, how to properly record, and conduct worthy studies and experiments.

○ For new users, present video explanations of why we want to be honest when uploading information onto our Make It Count profiles. Show examples of people performing positive specific attributes during work and school show examples of situations that would disqualify ourselves from specific attributes and why we don't want to lie or pretend we earned and performed attributes every day that we didn't just to inflate our ratings. Unless we do perform a lot of great attributes every day we should record it if we are trying to get our ratings up for a particular job or educational opportunity, but if we choose to consistently lie about some of our ratings just to qualify for greater opportunities, if we get that opportunity and don't perform as well as what we said we could do, then that won't look good on your next review; the truth will come out which makes performing good behavior lucrative and powerful for everyone. Detailed video tutorials describing how to use and take advantage of our applications and functions.

○ Create search lists of all educational facilities and all employers in the world who also have a Make It Count profile

○ Nearby zip code, school / employer search

○ List all nearby qualified schools and employers

○ Active resume viewer with editing tools and presentation capabilities so people can design their own custom resumes presentation with videos, pictures, and words that prove the lessons they have learned and experienced gained

○ List all current opportunities and offers available now

○ Create the passion school and career builder based on what the individual is passionate about and figure out how to empower the individual with all possible or a wide variety of steps any individual could take to become qualified for specific jobs and or educational opportunities that are available in your area. This tool is based on what the employer includes on the job description and based on what the individual has uploaded onto their public resume. This tool is the list of available employers and schools that teach the classes and experience that we may be interested in.

○ Create the not active or private historical resume proof page, which everything users upload that they want kept confidential. These would be experiences we see great value in, we want to record them for whatever reason, probably to use for a future opportunity that's not interesting in seeing or pursuing opportunities related to it at this time

○ As we start building these ideas, new ideas and obvious things that we need to do we can as we move forward

4. Design Employer Profile.

○ Employer name

○ Legal info

○ Overview Description

- ○ Profile Picture upload

- ○ Picture and Video uploads with editing capabilities for commercials and tours

- ○ Ask the employer to list all positions with experience needed and qualification descriptions

- ○ Highlight all available positions with job descriptions

- ○ Quick employee search with description, attribute, location filters

- ○ Quick opportunity distributer, describe available opportunity and create a filtered distribution list to send this opportunity directly to your target market, who you will know they are interested in a similar opportunity and or they match your search description

- ○ Individual profile viewer of qualified resumes that match employer search description, where you can view everything those individuals have experienced in their life time and uploaded it as a positive resume experience that employers like you might be interested in

- ○ As we start building these ideas new ideas and obvious things that we need to do we can as we move forward

5. Design Education Institute Profile.

- ○ Profile pictures

- ○ Descriptions

- ○ List of available classes, with teacher profile info attached

- ○ Positive Attribute average rating lists

- ○ Available teaching positions, with job descriptions and qualifications

- ○ Available student seats in all classes

- ○ Quick find Teacher / sub / students search and send opportunity, Description of opportunity, approximate dollar value range, minimum salary or hourly wage

- ○ People search engine, market available opportunity with link, qualified people may like and learn more on how to become a team member

- ○ Collect individual user referral fee

- ○ As we start building these ideas new ideas and obvious things that we need to do we can as we move forward

6. Design Professional Supervisor Profile.

- ○ Profile pictures

- ○ Description box

- ○ Employer pictures and description, with link

- ○ How many employees each day are being supervised, this week, last week, this month coming up, last month, last year, whole career, line graphs

- ○ How many employees have been trained, hired, fired, quit, line graphs

- ○ Opportunity sender

- Personal resume information just like the individual profile

- Individual employee rating list while under supervision with line graphs into the past to track improvements.

- Employee upload under review page, confirm button, pending request more proof and info button, denied button with reply box

- As we start building these ideas, new ideas, and obvious things that we need to do we can as we move forward

7. Design Teacher Profile.

- Profile pictures

- Description box

- Education institute pictures and description, with link

- How many students are being taught today, yesterday, last month, this month coming up, last year, whole career, with line graphs

- Personal profile information just like individual profile

- Individual student attributes and rating lists, with graphs

- Student upload page, confirm button, and request more proof and info button, denied description button with reply box

- As we start building these ideas, new ideas, and obvious things that we need to do we can as we move forward

8. Design Entrepreneur Profile.

- ○ Profile pictures

- ○ Description box

- ○ Project / module Description

- ○ Video documentary on how to properly document projects

- ○ Team builder page, experience / attribute rating preference's,

- ○ People search engine, market available opportunity with link qualified people may like and learn more and how to become a team member

- ○ Past projects / Descriptions, pictures and video documents upload

- ○ Personal resume profile just like individual program

- ○ Active resume viewer with editing tools and presentation capabilities like a 21st century PowerPoint program so people can design their own custom resume presentation with videos, pictures, and words that prove to the world what lessons they have learned and experienced gained.

- ○ As we start building these ideas, new ideas, and obvious things that we need to do we can as we move forward.

9. Design Agent Profile.

- ○ Create same as individual program

- ○ Add individual interlink capabilities to empower people acting as agents to connect opportunities together;

the agent profile can find employer and educational opportunities and present them to individuals who they think might be interested and if the agent helped put a deal together they can earn an income

10. Design Investor Profile.

　○ Create just like employer program

　○ Add share holder viewer; when individuals or entities who own stock in companies that are publicly traded and who want to participate, investors can view the positive attributes and experience their supervisors confirm

　○ Add graph and trend builder

11. Design Professional Athlete Recruiter Profile.

　○ Same as individual program

　○ Add athletic attributes and stats

12. Design Government Employee Recruiter Profile.

　○ Create just like employer program

　○ Each division of the government would need their own profile, local government positions, federal positions, this includes all legal government programs like the FDA, FBI, EPA, All military defense sectors, local police and fire fighters, etc.

　○ Quarterly public viewer trends that public and officials can review and publish

13. Interlink everything for everyone to search trends and data.
14. Apply a simple and fair monetary value for these services throughout the program except the individual profile, like other social media sites we want to enable anyone and everyone to participate in finding a job that they want for free, and see that particulars employers requirements for that job, and find the classes they can take to be qualified for the job they want, and see how they can earn scholarship money to pay for the classes they want to take. However depending on the schools there may be fees involved for their individual services.
15. Fair monthly packages and or functions can be purchased for all other profiles, and any other valuable functions we provide that have a great return of investment.
16. Create grants and scholarship prizes for people to earn.
17. As we start building these ideas, new ideas, and obvious things that we need to do we can as we move forward.

NOTES

CHAPTER

KEYS FOR FREEDOM

This module already exists in our world today so then the idea is to invest in businesses that are providing people with the highest quality information we can, practically any way we can, basically by creating a public funnel where everyone can go to learn and find answers via internet.

People having access to a healthy balance of information and education are what open pathways to more freedom. However, we must keep a balance and do our best to follow our hearts.

One of the parts to this idea I have is to picture is a mix between iTunes, YouTube, Ted-ed, Ted talks, and the Great Courses. A place that empowers legitimate teachers to be heard in long-form conversation and or with documentaries, from their personal testimony of what they believe they have learned about the subject. Including ideas and topics that maybe our education system isn't able to address fully because these are ideas on the leading edge coming from new discoveries, our teachers and students are having, informing the world in real-time. We will provide state of the art resources for teachers to be seen and rewarded as an artist does, but by publishing their video documentary teachings. Including the process for them to be herd and rewarded, creating a library of quality video documentary teachings creating the best place to find high-quality answers in the form of an informative video product course.

longbowhorseman@gmail.com

NOTES

CHAPTER

COMMUNITY PROJECT HOUSE

This fifth module is where a lot of our proceeds and capital that we gain from these other modules. Picture us building a new kind of college that brings the world together to learn hands-on lessons through community projects; where these main hub facilities are located they will need to be designed accordingly.

The main objective is to unite people together to work on projects that somehow help their whole community. Picture a combination between church, school, and scout camp. The point is to bring people together to communicate, seek to understand each other and love one another. We will do this by applying hands-on lessons through community projects, working as a long-term grassroots strategy that promotes fundamental traditions that are required to not only survive on this planet but learn how to thrive!

Our first project starts by purchasing pieces of land that can be turned into **community gardens.** We will need the proper facility and resources to send our staff/missionaries, people who want to serve somewhere in the world to find hungry people and bring them back to the garden. Where we will talk to them and learn things about each other and help each other with other things going on, while at the same time working with our hands learning how to grow food and prepare meals. Eventually, they will go out, teach and feed hungry people. We will work together with them in the garden,

longbowhorseman@gmail.com

learning together and teaching hands-on lessons together with the best we can.

At the main campus is where potentially millions of staff members and students will work together to facilitate every community project all over the world. Upfront, there will be a lot of arranging resources for many locations, but we can get a head start by partnering with property owners, businesses, and people who are already investing in the same community project. So, see if these people want our help, manpower, money, and resources to teach the people in their community the lessons involved in the project. When we are building new community projects from scratch it depends on what we have to work within the environment and what is a safe and smart investment for that area.

We would need to teach the missionaries beforehand at our home campus everything they need to know except being fluent in the local language; the Language barrier is obviously up to the individuals talking. And the beautiful part about working with someone hands-on in the garden to learn how to survive on this planet, we can both learn to understand each other much better. So, our missionaries need to be at least prepared to successfully take care of a variety of different fruits and vegetable plants related to the region, including how to preserve and prepare a healthy meal regularly. So, inside every facility, we would supply a kitchen with cookware, store basic ingredients and lesson plans. If no one on the front knows how to teach the necessary lesson we can use the Internet to help teach, especially in different languages in the form of state of the art video instructional information products.

The main objective every day will be getting the locals involved in as much of the process as they can, so people who live in that community can stop by whenever they want, get involved and help with the project; just do our best to keep the project moving forward. So, whenever we can, as missionaries we will want to be spending our time socializing with locals trying to make friends and see if some of them want to help out with their community projects.

When people come to our gardens it will be like going to church and school you will have to do some work and there will usually be a lesson involved and by the end, we will have learned how to grow fruitful relationships with each other while enjoying eating healthy food.

When we find people to come back with us to the garden as missionaries we don't always necessarily need to say very much. At first simply by going out to find hungry people who want to better themselves and provide a meal for themselves and their friends and family is the greatest project of them all, sometimes that is all that needs to be done. After we help people nourish their bodies if they want to come back and help, we can continue to grow our friendships. Over time, we will both grow hungry for more knowledge, as our fruitful relationships grow and the more good questions we continue to ask each other, so will the good answers.

As missionaries we will want to try and enlighten the people in the garden to try and have a good attitude, feeling and sending joyful vibrations while working and teaching lessons together. Because focusing on good things we love about life is like planting fruitful seeds in our mind. By focusing our thoughts around good ideas and then choosing to physically pay the price.

The whole point is to just do the best we can and work together so we can find more time to enjoy the fruits of our labors. Farming, gardening, raising livestock, hunting, fishing, forging, all done as respectfully as we can, and properly harvest, store, and prepare meals properly is one of the best ways to feel the great Spirit of life.

Over time those people will start to wonder about us as missionaries and start asking personal questions and that is when we can start to bare our personal testimonies and listen to people express themselves and build deep relationships with people all over the world.

That's what has to happen for more people who seem vastly different from each other to come together and learn how to love one another. By practicing good communication skills especially in person over long periods is how we grow to understand each other, which grows our love for one another. So, we all must spend time speaking from our hearts and empathetically listen to each other. We should practice interacting with each other more in person because while we are here in these bodies it's time to enjoy interacting physically with each other. However, learning how to communicate all the other technological ways is also important.

After we establish thriving community gardens all over the world the community project house will grow to create more advanced projects with the same mentality. For example, the next big project will be to figure out how to create a process to fund and implement a public Space and Science program built in our government and education system called Reach For The Stars, where students can choose to participate in advanced science projects and/or qualify to start their own project, if it somehow benefits the whole community. After we approve the project there will be a lot of real-life math and science subjects our teachers can use to teach our students hands-on and directly apply any possible lesson in a real-life project. That is the point of the Community Project House; to project and find lessons we can teach students hands-on in real life as much as possible so our children can see what they are learning to be applied with their own hands. The project will have plenty of time to get everything done, the projects main concern isn't how long it takes but that the project gets done exactly right the first time and everybody learns as much and teach as many subjects and students as we can throughout the whole process.

Depending on the circumstances the lessons might be limited at first but over time they will grow. For example, if a garden is thriving and local people in the community want to learn how to hunt wild animals for food, the missionaries in that area can qualify for whatever resources are available to go on a hunting adventure in a prepared fashion, execute, and preserve the hunted animals as respectful as possible. Or if they want to learn how to farm and raise domesticated animals, the garden can qualify to buy land and everything they need to respectfully help grow animals for food, in a manner that teaches the locals in that community what it takes to raise animals for food.

One of the main points of the community project house is to empower our education system with a proactive way to teach more hands-on, get our kids excited to discover intelligence and enlightenment. Use our available resources to get people involved in learning about better ways to take care of ourselves, each other, all lives on our planet, including how we can live in harmony with our environment.

NOTES

CHAPTER 8

THE RULES BEHIND CURRENCY

In God We Trust. What does that mean to you? To me, it means to trust in each other, because that's how we show trust in God; then we will learn that trust is more powerful than money.

The root of our money problems are complicated and run deep within our current ways of life. To heal this problem the right way is simple and it can be done. So, let's identify the root of this problem and go into the importance of currency including some of the **rules** behind it.

First, should start off saying Love is the ultimate transferable currency. Love is the most powerful currency throughout all dimensions of life. You can't lose if you love unconditionally, it's like being able to apply absolute value symbols around our life's equations and guarantee to see positive results.

There is a lot of people affected by every deal/transaction we make, and most of the people who are receiving money from the transactions we make we don't personally know that well or we don't get the chance to fully understand the influence our transactions will create. That's the risk we are all making in the economic world we have built today. We are all greatly dependent on each other to perform the P.L.U.R.R. principles in order to survive and thrive in our world today and that is where we find the power of trust in God. We are accountable for what our money fuels, therefore, we should seek to understand how the things we are purchasing come about, understand supply and demand and make sure it is worth the cost both spiritually and financially.

If we study the history of money and think about how money works we can recognize how some of the rules behind the money are a form of religion. When we think about that for a minute we can see how that is true. That means if we are planning on working for money our whole lives like so many of us do then we should consider understanding the rules to earn money and also pay attention to what our taxes are being spent.

Just like any other religion, many things about it make perfect sense and we can apply the rules to our lives; like knowing the difference between buying an asset and a liability. But then there's a whole bunch of financial products that get made up and thrown in the game that don't make sense, like derivatives, and financial products that take away people's wealth, and who knows what else?

The thing about currency is we need money to flow between us to participate peacefully in the economies we have created. We prefer money to flow between us to empower our peaceful ways of life.

One of our collective problems with money is the fact that at the end of the day all the energy that is created by all our collective hard work doesn't get reinvested the right way. Most of the worlds' energies and hard work gets diminished at the end of the day. This fiat system probably could work if at the end of the day the rules were designed to empower the fundamental things for life to grow which is applying the P.L.U.R.R. principles.

An example of how simple we could make sense of our money would be to hold our biggest banks accountable for the consequences of their investments.

When we research more on this topic, we can learn a lot about how our economies fundamentally work and see how specific rules have been used in the past. To understand it's possible to change the rules behind currency is to study history, you will see the rules behind currencies change all the time; some of the big changes for us in the

U.S. was in the mid-1800s after a civil war, another change came after the rise of our Industrial Age in 1913, creating the federal reserve bank. There were many changes throughout the world wars, and into the 1960s, and then finally the big game-changer happened in 1971, we saw one in 2008. We can see how it's time for another change.

I want to mention that there is still a lot of good that can come out of our current world fiat currency like the one we have today, and that's because pretty much all of us are good people if it didn't make some sort of sense it wouldn't have so much power. The best part is we are still given a choice of how to make and spend our money. It comes with a whole bunch of games we can play if we educate ourselves enough to learn how to play these games we can earn a lot of money to create a lot of amazing things for ourselves and others.

However, there needs to be a reevaluation of the entire financial sector, the stuff that makes sense will stay true, the rest is going to burst like a bubble.

NOTES

CHAPTER 9

POLITICS

The best analogy I can think of to help people realize how government and politics should work is to understand the game of golf. You see the reason why people like playing golf so much is because it's simple to understand how to play, the rules make sense, and the obstacle course is a beautiful mix between man, nature, and physics.

How we can relate golf to real life and politics is by understanding how to build a good golf course. Think about the course golf is played on. There are key built-in infrastructure projects or field markers that are indicators on how and where to play the game, and naturally, everyone can understand how to play and we all have similar tools with similar goals, strategies, and direction.

Think about when we start walking up to the tee box. Just off the path, there is a nicely groomed perched up Tee box with a beautiful view with markers pointing in the direction you want to hit the ball. There's a map of the area, and sometimes a jug of free water, lol, standing on the tee box and taking our first big swing in this metaphor would be like starting our day off at home with food, water, transportation, and once we take off on our journey to work or school, sometimes that is a long drive that lands nicely in an educational scholarship or well-paid career "far way", groomed nicely for our next shot, sometimes after our big shot we land in bad terrain like the long grass, weeds, sand traps, those represent bad jobs, getting into debt, and paying for college with debt or by yourself. The second shot we have to take is also a long term strategic choice that we need to make to give us another long leap forward, but this choice comes from a more technical position which is like our detailed duties at work and school. This second fairway shot could represent our career or educational choices that get our ball way down the fare way, hopefully, headed right close to your goal. Getting our ball on the green is a big accomplishment like earning a paycheck and bringing it home to take good care of your family. This is called the short game in golf when we are real close to where we want to be, but it's not always easy and technical on how well we finish, and how well we enjoy doing it again tomorrow.

Swinging the club to hit the ball is like choosing in the present moment which happens quickly and if we use our skills correctly like applying good principles in our lives is how we make good contact with the ball. Depending on which direction we are facing, how well we use the skills we have available to us, and if we can keep our head still while swinging at the ball;if we live on a golf course it will likely land on a nicely groomed fairway perched up looking good for our next big choice, ultimately getting closer and closer to achieving our daily and long term goals.

Making good choices sounds simple just like golf is easy to understand, especially when we know how to use our tools. We can feel confident to walk right up to our ball and just swing it. Hopefully, if you kept your head still, your ball will go relatively in the right direction. That's because you're playing a game that makes sense on a beautiful course that fundamentally guides us with empowerment to see all the possible opportunities available. We don't know where exactly our ball will land but at least we know we are headed in the right direction.

I think it's fair to say there is a bit of a delusion upon our people. The delusion I'm referring to is the political paradigm that exists in the United States. What I mean by that is how the two- political party system is segregating the American people. A clear example of that is when third-party/independent candidates aren't included in the official debates. The issues chosen to talk about, the questions asked, and lengthening the time restrictions for these debates is critical to understanding who the best candidates are we should vote for.

It makes sense to give definitions to categorize the kinds of choices we make, like liberal and conservative, but it doesn't make sense that we automatically divide our government and our people with unclear ideologies derived from their political parties' agenda which happens to be the polar opposite from each other. Making good choices in our government have nothing to do with being a republican or democrat, liberal or conservative. Many of us have been fooled by these strictly controlled ideological conversations.

This campaign to build these modules turns our governments into beautiful golf courses that are all uniquely different but still make sense for everybody to play the game we call life in harmony with our environment.

NOTES

CHAPTER

THE MILITARY INDUSTRIAL COMPLEX

World peace, creating defense jobs for survival and freedom to build our kingdoms how ever we want that makes sense today and for our children tomorrow; starts by increasing the contracted profit margins for defense manufacturers and government contractors to build **non-lethal rescue** natural disaster applications. We also need to build public publishing platforms that publish research into products and specific company policies, and practices that are, who are seriously harming life in our environment.

We can start to introduce many of these applications by mandating all government vehicles that have lethal applications must also come with a non-lethal rescue / natural disaster application.

Some examples,

- ☐ Vehicles with weapons like cannons must be designed to be interchangeable with non-lethal applications, like hydraulic arms that take many different attachments like a standard excavator claw.
- ☐ 51% government vehicles must come with applications that make it prepared to respond effectively to rescue people during natural disaster scenarios.
- ☐ All able body military personnel must be trained and empowered to respond to perform rescue missions during natural disasters.

- ☐ All United States Military vehicles and personnel must be equipped and be able to respond appropriately to save people in all likely possible scenarios on land, underground, in the ocean, on the coasts, in our sky, and from outer space.
- ☐ All United States military commanding officers can and maybe required to perform studies that somehow prove to protect the people and report honestly their findings on a public publishing format.

These applications can include learning and discovering our environments using science-based exploration and studies that are properly recorded as public information. That means a lot of applications will come from approved areas of study that are in the best interest of humanity. Like protecting the air we breathe, our freshwater supplies, life on land, in the soil, in our lakes and ocean. These applications will need to include proof of concept and include hands-on instructional training. All studies will need to be recorded as public information as honestly as we can. Every individual participants must give their honest perspective and in most cases by using the scientific method.

This policy is how we can all invest in our troops to have more positive experiences while serving the people; by qualified officers properly conducting pre-approved scientific studies and publishing the findings as public information as honestly as possible is how our troops can better protect everyone back home from enemies, both foreign and domestic. By conducting honest scientific studies collecting facts and evidence of our reality to inform the people on an open transparent public format of how they can protect themselves from harm; is the battlefield in the Information Age.

The range of training stays as it is, it depends on the branch of military people decide to volunteer in, land, underground, air, sea, outer space; not only will our troops be prepared to defend our country with lethal action if need be, but most of the time they will have spent serving themselves and the people in good ways that turn people into assets both during and after their service-employment.

By exploring and discovering all kinds of important things about protecting life is what it means to be a good warrior/ protector for your people. Imagine if the vast majority of people who serve us and who we serve come back home with a lot of amazing experience and stories to tell, including being able to know how and where to apply their valuable skills they learned from their service deployment.

If you join the Air Force you will get to learn about the sky and all that fly.

The Army will learn about protecting human life on land, and how to protect our soil, and learn about all the plants, and animals.

Marines will be responsible for protecting our lakes and rivers, shorelines.

The Navy will explore, protect, and preserve life that lives above and in the oceans, and on shorelines.

Government officials will be expected to investigate/study into any other official or commanding officers published work, and any commanding officer can investigate into any government officials' campaign. If the officer collects enough evidence of any products or policy that is seriously harming the people and life in their environment, then we the people expect the government officials and commanding officers to go to the front lines of our Information Age by publishing their findings honestly in order to keep there sworn duty to protect people from foreign and domestic enemies trying to cause serious harm. All other government and private programs like the FBI, CIA, NSA, and all the rest will always be subject to internal investigations by any commanding office in the United States Armed Forces or government officials who contain evidence to get multiple Judges to sign off on it will be able to conduct their own investigation and publish their findings.

This policy should naturally be what happens in our world today, especially when there are serious crimes against humanity being committed. When people volunteer to serve and protect us the people and eventually learn the skills necessary to do just that, then we should empower them to do just that, and then listen to what they have to say.

LEGISLATION DRAFT, BILL PROPOSAL

Long Bow Horse Man Enterprise
The United States Military Industrial Complex Act

This bill greatly empowers all good parts of our military-industrial complex and directs at least 51% of the current budget and capabilities towards real natural disaster threats. All real national security threats mean most applications must be designed to save lives during and after natural disasters.

These applications will be rewarded to companies who invent and can prove it works, and produce the required amount if so they can be approved for appropriate bonuses at the end of a successful contract not exceeding 100% gross cost.

This bill mandates at least 51% of the time and money spent on every individual soldier is applied towards science-based learning about critical aspects to protecting life in their local area because that is a lot of responsibility we can divide the natural parts of life-related to the branch of the government people volunteer to serve in. So, for example, if we choose to volunteer for the Army, the subject matter is narrowed down to learning everything we can about how to protect life on land. For example, every soldier in the army would learn about life in soil, ways to harness natural resources responsibly, study all life that exists especially the plants and animals that live in the local ecosystem, in the Navy you would learn everything about life on the coasts and in the oceans and how to prevent humanity from harming life in our oceans the best we can; the Air Force would be about protecting the air we breathe including learning everything about our skies and all that flies which includes many different insects that fly. Those of us who want to learn astrology and or be Astronauts would learn how humanity can survive with our reach beyond our planet, so for example, mining asteroids and moving them into safe zones, develop other places humanity can live to survive our earth's natural disasters; the idea is by passing legislation that keeps tax dollars flowing to our greatest manufacturing asset and job creator but mandate we all start developing non-lethal natural disaster applications and fund public knowledge expeditions based on critical issues.

By applying these ideas, we can wake our sleeping giant again, work together with all nations to save our world by turning our destructive forces into positive growth and survival of our civilization.

The rest of the time will involve our defense duties but if no significant threat exists because fewer assets are doing the job, then all other Commanding Officers can be assigned or create missions to study life, teach, learn, explore, and publicly record their studies for the people back home to learn from as well.

This combats false information that could be used to harm people. For example, anyone will be able to research what our military has discovered, see the real facts about critical information that can keep people safe and live in harmony with their environment. Every study will report all evidence as public information, building a critical fact-checker against other information being published. For example, some companies that sell useful products may also have harmful things about the product; if our military deems it necessary they can perform a scientific study and publish their findings to protect people from harm. So our soldiers will serve themselves and the people in many ways on the front lines in this Information Age.

Our world's military industrial complex can build non-lethal applications that can save countless lives during and after natural disasters that are specific to each local county district. This exponentially expands the whole manufacturing industry because the private sector and local governments will be able to purchase many pre-approved natural disaster applications that can save people's lives during an emergency, especially for common weather patterns specific to the region.

This will create millions of new manufacturing jobs and stimulate the entire economy in many ways. Creating this pathway will naturally flow a great deal, more "natural" honest money to all the people who build our infrastructure. A base Minimum wage requirement will be applied, and the number of jobs created and/or potential lives saved will also be considered.

- Whereas, the military industrial complex creates a great deal of jobs in the world.
- Whereas, about half of the federal budget is already spent to fuel this industry in the way of national security and creating jobs.
- Whereas, natural disasters, effect individual States differently. This bill empowers local governments to apply for and design their own natural disaster applications and find the things they need to reinforce their local infrastructure.
- Whereas, many lethal applications are now useless or senseless for the battlefield, and now they are a huge liability just taking up space. These types of applications can be traded out for non-lethal applications that may qualify for higher profit margins.
- Whereas, much of the manufacturing processes to produce non-lethal natural disaster applications is basically the same process as manufacturing defense applications.
- Whereas, stockpiling weapons for war is costly and produces great amounts of toxic waste.
- Whereas, the irony of creating weapons of massive destruction has technically comes with a stale mate.

- Whereas, it is the duty of a warrior for good to protect life in his or her environment.
- Whereas, The American people do not have a public space program there is a great opportunity for a non-lethal public space program.

By directing and empowering the military industrial complex in this way helps prevent the risk of mass destruction, and greatly serves humanity. The more this industry flows in this direction, the more this entire industry can grow.

This bill will create millions of amazing jobs and turn America back into a manufacturing super power.

NOTES

CHAPTER

LANGUAGE ARTS,
READING AND WRITING

When we study the past and read historical documents some of which are part of religions we know as scriptures. We can study these writings to gain insight into the past and learn from their experiences to make better choices in our lives today. Even with how different our lives are today than the people we are researching about, fundamentally, we have pretty much been the same for thousands of years. So, when we read what are hand-written journal entries from people expressing what they are feeling, or recording something about their lives means we can likely learn from their story with our imaginations. Even if the story was changed as it was translated and passed down, anything that people have left behind is valuable information we can use to travel through time today and build better present and future life experiences.

Reading, writing, keeping a hand-written journal for ourselves and recording things about our life in meaningful ways that are true will help us understand how to interpret other people's writings, especially ancient journal texts and scriptures. I believe we should read, write, watch TV, use technology, live in our environment with awareness to learn from all that we can and somehow figure out how to use what we come across to further enlighten ourselves and others so we can continue finding further joy and live more positive experiences, especially if we like exploring the world.

There are a lot of amazing places and beautiful people waiting to be discovered out there and every one of them is beautiful in their own way. If you believe that is true then we should spend at least some of our times doing our part to better understand each other's cultures, beliefs, and different ways of life. That means if we believe in practicing the P.L.U.R.R. Principles we can continue to live in an environment where we can travel all over the world more often with joyful intent to explore our different ways of life. In the garden is the best place to come together, to learn about each other and fall in love with each other and find beauty in our differences, especially in our food.

CHAPTER

AGRICULTURE, CONSTRUCTION, MINING, RECYCLING, WILDLIFE, ELECTRICITY

From what I have discovered we have made great collective success in these fundamental parts of our life, more in some parts of our world than others.

How we can all show more responsible practices in these activities can be figured out by peacefully uniting together and respectfully listening to all responsible parties and then figure out the best investment to unite good parts from all responsible plans until the problem is figured out or solved on an open public platform.

By respectfully listening to all parties when it comes to how we should better live in harmony with wildlife, I am especially referring to our Native American brothers and sisters. Why we should listen and learn from them, you should already know especially if you celebrate Thanksgiving every year. Why we must listen to responsible Native American people is because they have the deepest roots in this soil. There is no doubt their ancestors shed the most blood sweat and tears for this land. And when we understand the Native American cultural knowledge and traditions we can learn how to live in harmony with the Great Spirit. Especially to understand how we can apply P.L.U.R.R. Principles with Mother Nature's wildlife.

We all need efficient and stable big agricultural practices where there are a lot of people, mixed with local farmers growing a wide variety of plants and animals that can thrive in the conditions of the area. That is why we want to invest in community gardens to help educate people about the best ways to grow food with what we have to work with. The Health Care Act Bill proposes we can create a high-grade food supply that doctors and pharmaceutical companies and everybody can start investing in. That is another way we can build a stable high-quality food market that anyone who desires to be a legit farmer can become qualified to participate in this market. This will create a more stable high-quality food market where farmers can earn a more predictable profit for specialty grown food. This may empower anyone to be able to get the license in order to even grow just a small amount of high quality food that doctors may have a demand for in the area, where everyone can earn a good profit for growing high-quality food and making it available to the top-dollar guaranteed pharmacy market which is also directly connected to the entire food market, just like we connect pharmaceutical drugs with our grocery stores.

I am starting to get some experience in learning mining, geology, chemistry, metallurgy, smelting, refining, casting, welding, and recycling. Understanding these works and arts are critical to becoming one with our environment. I will eventually propose to implement small scale mining operations all over the world that locals can go to learn these works of art practices, I plan on rolling this out through the Community Project House.

Recycling what we have already taken from the earth is wise. Knowing what to do with what resources we have available around us is where we can find a great deal of hidden capital that we can all find and figure out how to re-use to build our kingdoms in our world today. Creating Recycling modules means we will make all materials that can be recycled worth something and available to the market to figure out what to do with.

When we are constructing our homes and commercial real estate naturally we should consider how we can live in harmony with our environment, this means we should consider creating more underground architecture, understand the local wildlife more and build migratory paths where we are affecting other species.

I am excited to share these words about electricity with you. So, we can better understand the significance of what we call "electricity, light, stars, our sun". Which happens to be the light body of scientific evidence and symbol for "God" our hire power, our source energy, and unite science and religion in our world today.

Think about the difference between us being alive or dead? It is the electrical current flowing through our bodies. We can prove that when our heart goes into cardiac arrest…! shockingly we can come back to life.

Think about what people have said during near death experiences and what light they have in common?

Think about all the different written historical accounts of people explaining what it was like encountering an Angelic being or experiencing God? We can go all the way back to some parts of Ancient Egypt - they worshiped the Sun, Greeks- Zeus controlled lightning, In all the Abrahamic religions there are many written records of people experiencing God and Angels and they all usually have light associated in the story.

Think about how Science – understands how to wield electricity to create basically all things, but science doesn't know how to explain what electricity actually is? We know our world is electrically charged because we can observe lightning storms and even create our own static charge inside our bodies, carry it around with us under the right conditions and then literally be like Zeus and electrically shock people we love.

Think about Religion and philosophy which is just as powerful and important as science to understand our source energy in the opposite, to empower us with what God is with faith, spiritual traditions, and stories that teach how and why we should shine our light and wield our electric powers to create good in our world today.

In our world today we are or can be extremely empowered with all kinds of electrical technology to build good things in our world today. Generator motors, batteries, resistors, capacitors, transistors, inductors, integrated circuits, transformers, precious metal wire, lightbulbs, vehicles, hv/ac, computers, lasers, communication, internet, satellites, the sun, the earths electrical field, our human brain, all of these electrical devices simply add up and simply reduce to prove "God" is our source energy, all powerful, all knowing, and enlightening our world all the time today.

WAYPOINTS

- Publish a book to find investors
- Build a team for FWM
- Spread the FWM strategy through supporting schools and event centers all over the world.
- We can develop our own patented biodegradable water bottle and or partner with many water bottle manufacturers and suppliers to be our distributors.
- Create the Rent a Bike device.
- Develop health insurance agency partnerships.
- Sell health insurance as I described with the rental bike process.
- Work with public transportation authorities.
- Roll out Rent a Bike everywhere by leasing out our devices to individuals and local bike shop owners and bicycle manufactures.
- Explain the Make It Count program to a team of computer programmers; create a demo program to see how it will work.
- Immediately start coding this program.
- Communicate what this program will do for our world economies and what life will be like after we roll it out with our education systems.
- Right away we will want to work with existing community garden leaders and offer them our help and services and also purchase pieces of land all over the world that can be used for our community garden project.

- Prepare to accept and arrange many community projects.
- Where ever people are these modules will grow, and the world will be a far better place with these modules in our lives.
- Keep planting those seeds and many others that follow the P.L.U.R.R. principles all over the world.

longbowhorseman@gmail.com

MY RESUME

For those of you who are thinking about getting involved and want to know more about me and get to know me personally, I would love to meet with you. I want to empower you with opportunities involved with this campaign which is creating a world where not only you but everyone can succeed and do whatever you want with your life. I would love to empower you with a great way to earn a lot of money by playing an important role in serving humanity, by being responsible for saving the good in our civilization.

The Long Bow Horse Man Enterprise is the name of my holding company, - Long stands for the long term, and the test of time, Bow stands for innovation, technology, Horse stands for mastering our environment, understanding ideologies, Man stands for all of our humanity, Enterprise stands for the undertaking of difficult projects and building business modules to show a real collective responsibility.

Here is a little bit about me and some of my resume.

First of all, I want to make sure everyone understands I am not perfect; of course, I have made a lot of mistakes. I consider myself to be average at a lot of things.

The present year is 2018, I am 27 years old and I am deeply in love with Darci Earl, we have two children and one dog Leo. Darci is 26, Adalynn is 2, Baylin is almost 1, and Leo is a 45lbs Australian Shepard Blue Healer mix.

We love going on adventures together as a family and with friends, especially exploring life in the mountains. We love exploring the public library, public lands, and experiencing all of the different walks of life with expressed art forms throughout our cities.

I was born into a loving family in Bountiful, Utah, on November 26, 1990. The ideological cultural background I grew up in and still somewhat influenced by the workings of Christian ideologies and living in Utah; that is mostly done by members of the Church of Jesus Christ of Latter-day Saints. I did choose to be a member of this church when I was eight years old. However, in my early teens, I became less active because I didn't want to identify with a group apart from everyone else. My concern as a kid was making as many friends as I could, I didn't know who I was as a teenager very well but I was able to make it through hard times because of some of the things I learned from Christianity and the LDS Church. I figured out early on the teachings of Jesus "the truth" is easy to understand but it can be made seem complex and confusing. Christianity can be understood with one sentence. It's known as the golden rule. *"Do unto others as you would have them done unto you."* That is how I try to live my life.

I realized early on if I wanted to make the world a better place I better go where my heart and the wind take me; where ever I end up, I better learn from my experience, especially learn from my mistakes. As time passes, we can look back and keep learning new lessons from our experience. Then somehow, we can turn our experienced knowledge into wisdom by passing along what my experience has taught me to a friend or family member as honestly as I can, converse in ways that we learn and tend to practice what we talked about; I believe is a good way we can learn from our mistakes and peruse ways to better our lives and the lives around us.

My great grand parents were farmers and ranchers, so we all kinda grew up helping out around the farm the best we could because we also all went to school, played sports, and worked other jobs. We definitely earned a lot of good hard working memories that come with running a family farm. We were fortunate enough to be able to purchase some grazing rights up in Ashely forest where we would drive 300+ cows on horse back. We would be on back of a horse for days pushing through the most beautiful wilderness terrain, I must admit the reality is of course it's not easy keeping track of hundreds of cows kick-in up dust, plus all the hollering the cows make, all the hooting and hollering us grandkids make to keep the cows in line, and especially the hoot-in and hollering the grandparents make to keep us kids in line:) There is no other work more satisfying then cowboying a horse all day through beautiful wilderness leading some of Mother Nature to a heavenly promise land with family and friends.

I had an amazing childhood; I was always surrounded by loving family and friends. However, in my teenage years, I have been prescribed with the drug Accutane, to help cure my acne which it did, but it came with horrible effects, the sun burns I'd get were severely painful, mood swings especially because I was going through puberty at the same time. After a second cycle, I became seriously confused and depressed. During or shortly after that same time, I was prescribed with pain pills for sports injuries and right away I became addicted to opioids early in my life until I finally made it to a behavioral rehabilitation practice called Odyssey House.

It was during my time in that program when I became enlightened. It was early in the program but after many group therapy sessions where I empathetically listened to other people tell their life stories and after a few times of my butt being in the hot seat, dumping my insides out in front of other people as honestly as possible, is how I became enlightened; by empathetically listening and speaking honestly from my heart I was able to learn a great deal about myself in a short amount of time. I learned how to look at myself and my behavior honestly, look at the bad habits I want to change, which then starts to enlighten the dark path I was on; now I can see the way I want to go.

MY PROFESSIONAL RESUME
EXPERIENCE SUMMED UP

Age 16, summer of 2006, Tooele City Parks and Rec. - I helped take care of local parks, picked up garbage, cleaned graffiti, mowed lawns, put together the stage for local events, and drove around town in the city truck. Great first job, I have great memories and stories from that summer.

Age 17, Tooele City Golf Course - Mowed roughs, mowed around tee box to fare way, picked up garbage, filled in divots, and played a lot of golf for free.

Age 18, Full-time High School - starting varsity football QB, I had completed 60 college credits for general associates.

Age 19, Part-time Forklift Lead for a Pallet Manufacture in the Tooele Industrial Depot

Part-time Aviation Classes at Utah Valley University

Age 20-21, Full-time Lead in Pallet Manufacture, - I learned many key aspects to running a wood manufacturing company. I was also being mentored by the General Manager, Craig, who taught me about business and manufacturing shipping products out of wood. We did have awesome machinery to empower us to do the job but it was very difficult and labor-intensive. I was very fortunate because most of our team members were Mexican people. They were awesome to work with. I love getting to know them and sharing blood sweat and tears with those guys for 3 years. It was a great cultural learning experience for me. We busted our butts every day in the hot sun and the freezing winter months, it didn't matter these guys always showed up for work and did their best all day every day. I gained a great deal

longbowhorseman@gmail.com

of love and respect for my Mexican coworkers and their culture; I learned a great deal about business and manufacturing products from wood /shipping products. Thanks to the GM, at the time my first mentor, who I owe a great deal of my knowledge and experience.

This is also the year when I started to uncover the Free Water Marketing business module.

Age 21, is when Darci and I met; quickly fell deeply in love I needed a steady income so I could be approved for a mortgage, so I decided to do what my grandpa did, go see if I can get a stable job with good benefits in the defense industry manufacturing in Salt Lake. At the place I was hired, they were primarily a defense contractor manufacturing parts with carbon fiber using state of the art machines and technology. I was hired as an expediter for production control. We scheduled production and tracked all parts along the process to ship. We were responsible for expediting all tools, material and shop orders. All the tools had to be moved with forklifts and cranes, we did everything we can to make sure parts get out on time which requires us to keep good relationships with a lot of people in every stage of production, we learned a little bit about every step in manufacturing and I gained a good broad insight into the defense contractor manufacturing industry. We also made a lot of spreadsheets.

Age 22, this year 20% of employees were laid off from defense contractor I was one of them, however, they called me back a month later to work as a shipping associate for less money. I liked my coworkers, I was desperate for a steady income to invest in my first primary residence, so I took the pay cut so I could close the real estate deal and started learning about shipping. I also took out my first FHA mortgage on a little house in South City, Salt Lake. I formed FWM into an LLC and practiced my hand at being a part-time salesman; I listened and read a lot of books especially ones written by Dale Carnegie, Stephen Covey, Robert Kiyosaki, Ester and Jerry Hicks, Napoleon Hill, Marcus Aurelius.

Age 23, I became the Lead Shipping Associate for the new programs at the new facility shipping hundreds of carbon fiber parts every day. I learned a great deal about how everything comes together to the customer's hands.

Age 24, I quit the defense industry and jumped in full-time to self-teach by reading and writing and thinking about my subjects a lot. I had a great desire to self-teach so I was going to the public library at downtown Salt Lake, one to two times a week and watched hundreds of nonfiction documentaries on a wide range of subjects; I learned a lot of amazing things in a short period. And I was able to build most of these modules in my head and write them down this year. Oh, and I got a lot of parking tickets.

I also made my first partner, Josh, who is a local Attorney; he has helped me work out these ideas a lot and he has been a great deal of moral support, listening to my work through these modules and helps put everything together.

Age 25, for a few months, I stayed at home to take care of Adalynn and started writing this book; reaching out to people and filling my head with knowledge from the Internet and the library.

I started working part-time commercial construction with one of my best friends growing up, Jordon, and his dad, Dennis, who is one of the best General Contractors in Utah; he was also one of my football coaches growing up. I learned a great deal about life and construction this year.

My little brother and I successfully flipped a hundred-year-old house and I was able to pay off all my debts.

As a family, we have been adventuring into the mountains often and prospecting public lands, hoping we can stake a mineral claim, so we can learn and practice the art of mining and metallurgy, and earn our capital from the Earth.

Age 26, Working for Dennis - we completed many successful construction projects as a Superintendent all over Utah. We worked in hospitals, restaurants, churches, banks, high-rises, apartment complexes, and hotels. We get to go to places where normally nobody ever gets to go. I have learned a great deal about life and construction and have gained a great deal of construction worker stories I would love to tell you about.

Darci and I birthed our second child, Baylin. He has been a delight; both of our kids are smart, growing healthy and strong.

Age 27, I am a construction worker, a Superintendent still working for Dennis. While at the same time, I can't wait to be an Author and publish these ideas, build an amazing team, and then build these modules all over the world.

Age 28, I am a published author / Construction worker/miner. - That's right, after many beautiful days of prospecting the mountains I have finally found a way I can learn the ways of being a prospector/ miner.

CLOSING STATEMENT

There you go, just like I said, beyond a doubt.

Now, in this present moment, if you even somewhat comprehended what you just read, then you know how to save our civilization. You now know the greatest return of investment strategy of our time. What are you going to do, now that you know how to save our civilization? If you were wondering what I am going to do with all the power of the universe that exists inside of me just like it has always existed inside of you, I am going to do my best to wield my powers peacefully. I want to love as much as possible, I believe I am that I am one with The universe, I will do my best to respect all and fear none, I will do my best to be responsible with my powers when I can respond to do something good.

I did leave out a lot of important strategic information on building these modules, of course, because it can't be explained correctly in a written format like this right now. A lot depends on what happens in my present moment, many things haven't happened yet. To understand the rest will require you to reach out to me with your questions. If you are interested but not sure what to think but you know it's the right thing to do to get involved, all you have to do is email us your information and let us know what you think about these ideas, and how would you like to help? We will reply with our current available opportunities and do our best to empower you in many ways.

Sincerely,
Christopher D Iorg
Email: longbowhorseman@gmail.com

CPSIA information can be obtained
at www.ICGtesting.com
Printed in the USA
BVHW041109200120
569969BV00009B/51